# Contents

# What are spacecraft?

Spacecraft are **vehicles** that go into space.

They can carry people and other things.

# Wheels, wings and water

# Spacecraft

## Heather Miller

**www.raintreepublishers.co.uk**
Visit our website to find out more information about **Raintree** books.

To order:
☏ Phone 44 (0) 1865 888112
▤ Send a fax to 44 (0) 1865 314091
▢ Visit the Heinemann Bookshop at **www.raintreepublishers.co.uk** to browse our catalogue and order online.

First published in Great Britain by Raintree, Halley Court, Jordan Hill, Oxford OX2 8EJ, part of Harcourt Education.
Raintree is a registered trademark of Harcourt Education Ltd.

Editorial: Charlotte Guillain and Diyan Leake
Design: Michelle Lisseter
Picture Research: Maria Joannou and Amor Montes de Oca
Production: Lorraine Hicks

Originated by Dot Gradations
Printed and bound in China by South China Printing Company

ISBN 1 844 21368 4 (hardback)
07 06 05 04 03
10 9 8 7 6 5 4 3 2 1

ISBN 1 844 21378 1 (paperback)
08 07 06 05 04
10 9 8 7 6 5 4 3 2 1

**British Library Cataloguing in Publication Data**
Miller, Heather
Spacecraft. – (Wheels, wings and water)
387.8
A full catalogue record for this book is available from the British Library.

**Acknowledgements**
The publishers would like to thank the following for permission to reproduce photographs: AP Wide World Photos, **11L**; Corbis, **11R**, **23** (capsule); Corbis/AFP, **8**; Corbis/James L. Amos, **9**; Corbis /NASA/Roger Ressmeyer, **5**, **19**; Corbis/Roger Ressmeyer, **6**; Corbis/NASA, **20**, **23** (astronaut), backcover; NASA, **7**, **10**, **22**, **24**; NASA Langley Research Center, **17**; Summer Productions, **21**; TRIP/NASA, **14**; Visuals Unlimited/A. J. Copley, **16**; Visuals Unlimited/NASA/Science VU, **4**, **15**, **18**, **23** (vehicle and launch pad); Visuals Unlimited/Science VU/NASA/JPL, **13**; Visuals Unlimited/Scott Berner, **12**

Cover photograph of spacecraft, reproduced with permission of NASA/Kennedy Space Centre.

Every effort has been made to contact copyright holders of any material reproduced in this book. Any omissions will be rectified in subsequent printings if notice is given to the publishers.

Some words are shown in bold, **like this**. You can find them in the glossary on page 23.

**Astronauts** fly some spacecraft.

Some spacecraft go into space without people inside.

# What do spacecraft look like?

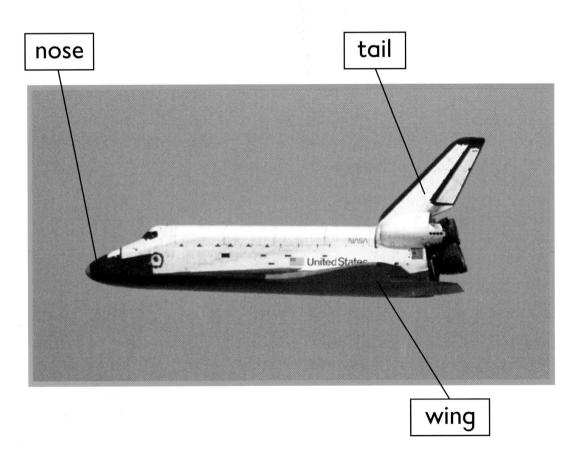

nose

tail

wing

Some spacecraft look like **jets**.

They have a nose, wings and a tail.

Rockets look like tall tubes.

They have tops shaped like cones.

# What are spacecraft made of?

Parts of spacecraft are made of metal.

Other parts are made of different materials.

tiles

Some spacecraft are covered
with special tiles.

They keep the spacecraft safe
from heat.

# How did spacecraft look in the past?

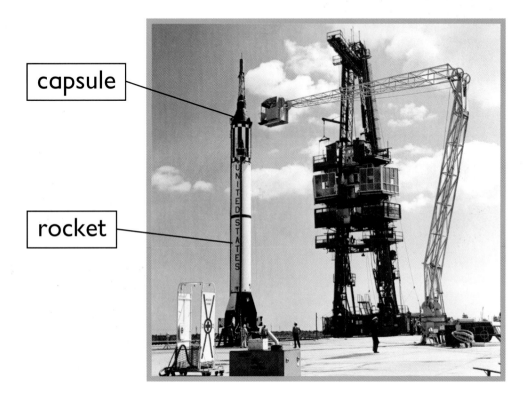

capsule

rocket

Early spacecraft were small **capsules**.

Capsules were sent into space on big rockets.

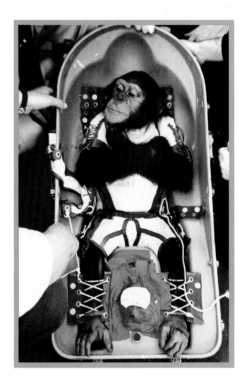

The first capsules carried animals.

Later, capsules carried just
one **astronaut**.

# What is a rocket?

A rocket pushes a spacecraft into space.

A rocket is filled with **fuel**.

Fuel makes the rocket lift off from a **launch pad**.

Flames and smoke shoot out as the rocket launches.

# What is a space shuttle?

A space shuttle carries people and things into space.

It flies in space like a **jet**.

The space shuttle stays in space for a few days.

**Astronauts** then fly the space shuttle back to Earth.

# What is a rover?

A rover is a **vehicle** that can drive on **planets** and the moon.

This **astronaut** is driving a rover on the moon.

Some rovers do not carry astronauts.

This rover is looking at rocks
on the planet Mars.

# What is a space station?

A space station is a spacecraft that holds many **astronauts**.

It stays in space for a very long time.

Astronauts can live and work on a space station.

This astronaut is eating in space.

# Why are some spacecraft special?

Jetpacks are spacecraft that help **astronauts** move in space.

Astronauts wear jetpacks on their backs.

Probes are spacecraft that take pictures of **planets**.

People cannot ride in probes.

# Quiz

Do you know what kind of spacecraft this is?

Can you find it in the book?

Look for the answer on page 24.

# Glossary

**astronaut**
someone who travels from Earth into space

**capsule**
part of a spacecraft that holds the astronauts

**fuel**
material used to power something

**jet**
aircraft that moves using jet engines

**launch pad**
place that a spacecraft takes off from

**planet**
one of the large bodies in space that moves around a star. Our planet is the Earth.

**vehicle**
machine that carries people or things from place to place

# Index

Answer to quiz on page 22.
This is a rocket.